content

07 welcome to modblock

08 contributors

articles

10 the heart of form & function

14 create a quiet space to thrive

18 it's hip to be square

patterns

20 boxed wedge

28 cornerstone

36 moonlight

44 rhombus dance

52 light box

58 tiny wonky star

66 rising star

74 slice-a-block

82 twin sisters

90 modern courthouse

100 reference

form & function

▸ welcome to Modblock

Welcome to the second issue of Modblock. We're so excited to be back! The idea of form and function as our next issue sprang up naturally after pondering color. Taking the next step, we explored how the beauty of quilts interacts with the way we use them.

Quilting is different than many other art forms because it is so familiar and traditional. In fact, the wonderful quilting done by our ancestors has often been taken for granted because of those reasons, but we seek to bring out our treasured quilts from the attic, smooth them out, and take a closer look. There is love and creativity in every stitch. We can be inspired by them and make our own new traditions. There's no wrong way to go about it. Play with pattern, simplify, or even embellish, it's all up to you.

In this issue, we will talk about using negative space, simplified designs, and variations on traditional quilt blocks to create new forms. Our goal is to help you see existing patterns with new eyes, or venture into uncharted territory and try something entirely different. With simple techniques, a whole new world of possibilities can open up for you! We hope you love this issue of Modblock. Let's go create something beautiful together!

▶ Amy Ellis

Author of Think Big: Quilts, Runners, and Pillows from 18" Blocks, quilter, blogger, fabric designer for Moda Fabrics, wife and mom to four.
www.amyscreativeside.com

▶ Carrie Bloomston

Author of The Little Spark, professional artist, textile designer for Windham Fabrics, abstract painter, writer, teacher and yogi.
www.carriebloomston.com

▶ Christine Ricks

Creative Director for MSQC's Block & Modblock magazines and contributing modern quilt designer.
www.missouriquiltco.com

▶ Christopher Thompson

Known on social media as the_tattooed quilter. Modern quilt designer and lover of all things crafty.
www.thetattooedquilter.com

▶ Rob Appell

Host of Man Sewing on YouTube. His nature-inspired quilts are full of life, just like him! Check Rob out at:
www.mansewing.com &
www.robappell.com

▶ Ron Doan

Ron and his wife Jenny live in a small town in rural Missouri. He is a beloved father and grandfather. He enjoys mechanics, art, motorcycle riding, and quilting!

▶ Sara Gallegos

Divides her time between raising two daughters, her quilt shop, and teaching at Baby Lock Dealerships around the country. Watch her instructional videos at
www.sewathomeclasses.com

▶ Victoria Findlay Wolfe

Author of 15 Minutes of Play and Double Wedding Ring Quilts, Sizzix designer, Juki Ambassador, award-winning quilter, Harley-rider, wife, and mother.
www.vfwquilts.com

▶ Natalie Earnheart

Chief editor and contributing designer for Modblock & Block magazine www.missouriquiltco.com

▶ Jenny Doan

Jenny and her husband, Ron, love the rural life. She has a passion for quilting, teaching, and grandchildren! Jenny is the host of MSQC's quilting channel on YouTube. www.missouriquiltco.com

thank you

A big, heartfelt thanks to our wonderful contributors. We couldn't do this without you! This fantastic bunch of quilters have gathered together to help us bring you the latest issue of Modblock. They've inspired us with their creativity and we hope it sparks your imagination! There's a lot of love in these pages and it's been amazing to work with such passionate, imaginative people.

the heart of form & function

article by Nichole Spravzoff

Throughout history, quilting has been used for many diverse purposes: to keep warm, decorate homes, express political views, preserve memories, and so much more. Made by hand, often collaboratively—and using familiar materials such as scraps of clothing—quilts are personal, functional, and most of all beautiful.

form and function

The American architect Louis Sullivan coined the phrase "form follows function," and although we use it often, what does it really mean? The early roots of this idea are found in the writings of a Roman architect named Marcus Vitruvius who said that a structure should have three qualities—it should be solid, useful, and beautiful. That idea has been passed down through the years to our day. Sullivan's famous assistant, Frank Lloyd Wright, went even further to say, "Form follows function—that has been misunderstood. Form and function should be one, joined in a spiritual union." In quilting, this takes on a new meaning. Form and function are joined into one in this art form, a visual representation of comfort and love. Quilts are meant to be used and passed on from generation to generation. They are not kept under glass, but are cherished and worn threadbare.

the modern movement

Modern Quilting has adopted this adage well. As form follows function, we use up what others might leave behind. Our ancestors speak through their quilts, some of which have recently been recognized as important works of art. They gathered up faded calicoes, feed sack prints, treasured scraps of clothing, and worn work attire, stitching them together into quilts that came alive and spoke about

size matters

Maybe you're stuck in a rut with the traditional 10" square block. Think large—or even very small! Changing up the scale of a pattern can do wonderful things for quilts. Instead of stitching individual log cabin blocks, consider making the entire quilt as one large block. The results are quite impressive. Stagger large blocks with small ones and give your quilt variety. You'll have a lot of fun.

take a deep breath

Modern quilts often allow for plenty of "breathing room" in between blocks. Instead of evenly spaced rows, try making a quilt with a few accent blocks and allow the rest to remain solid fabric. Place the blocks off center or at a quirky angle.

their heritage. We seek to emulate their examples, finding inspiration in the everyday and expressing ourselves through the medium of fabric.

art or not?

Deciding whether or not quilting is an art form is largely a matter of opinion as their beauty is undeniable. Take the example of the Gee's Bend quilters in Alabama. When they were first approached about having their quilts displayed in

▶ ## challenge tradition

The next time you look at your grandmother's quilt, consider how you might create a similar pattern, but in your own way. There may be a simpler approach to a seemingly complex design.

improv exercises

If you wait for the mood to strike you, you may be waiting for some time. Instead of waiting, try playing! Grab a stack of neglected fabric, or a basket full of scraps and see what comes together. Don't shy away from cutting and piecing. You can always rearrange. Try new color combinations and let yourself clash. You might be surprised—and amazed—with what you come up with!

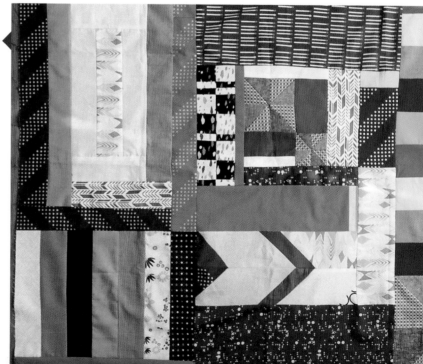

the Whitney Museum in New York, as well as other fine art museums nationwide, they had no idea that they had created something so unique and admirable, let alone something that would be viewed in a gallery. These quilts were made out of necessity, with their imaginations as their patterns. Now their work is viewed as some of the highest folk art ever created in America. Quilts that once graced humble beds now adorn the halls of grand museums.

Modern quilting seeks to embrace the traditional while introducing innovation and bold color, going beyond the expected. Variations on time-honored patterns can take on a life of their own, becoming abstract art. But as we consider this question of art or not, it seems to matter less how a quilt is made when we consider why it was made.

create contrast, or not?

Using intensely saturated or subtle color in a thoughtful manner can make all the difference. Squint at your quilt and look to see which spots of contrast really stand out, or use specialty glasses made to discern contrast. Pay attention to light and dark spots. Is it mostly a blur? Can you see the pattern emerge? Whatever your preference, make it yours—that's the true secret to all art.

the heart of quilting

At the heart of a love of quilting and sewing is the desire to create. The process of taking raw material and turning it into something wonderful evokes a deep sense of satisfaction. It is more than just putting together pretty scraps of fabric. It becomes a true reconciliation of form and function. It is art, yet it is usable in our daily lives. Quilts aren't just hung on walls, they're wrapped around our loved ones. They make our world beautiful and comfortable. In this sense, a quilt can even act an extension of ourselves, reaching out to touch the lives of those around us. That is the inner beauty of creating a quilt.

create a quiet space to thrive

article by Carrie Bloomston

When I sit down to paint, sew, or write, I'm often thinking about one thing that might surprise you: emptiness. Yep, negative space. Empty, quiet space is one of the most important parts of any design. As artists, quilters, and designers, we certainly want to create something real and tangible—maybe even fun and whimsical. We instinctively invade the negative space with our splashes, spills, stamps, and doodles. We go after the empty page or blank fabric with our good intentions of filling it up with love and joy—or whatever it is we have set out to create on our journey.

But how often do we stop to consider the space around our design? Without a sense of quiet, our work might become smothered, having no breathing room. When you listen to music, without a pause in between notes, you'd never hear the tune. We need these pauses in our work to make it impactful. The importance of negative space is addressed in formal composition. It's the idea that the space around the form is as important as the form itself because they work together. So how can we capture that feeling of quiet in our images?

We need to create a space for it to come into the quilted picture plane. We can start just by looking for negative space and recognizing it in our world.

Space and light are all around us. Gaze upward and notice the silhouette of branches against a bright, clear sky. See how shadows cut across the floor midday and how it transforms the room. When we honor the emptiness and quietude surrounding our images, we can give them their shining moment in the sun. Remember that we don't necessarily have

to fill up every single space in a composition with color or form. We need some place to just be—silent, muted, and hushed, like a snow covered field in winter. Empty space is just like light and air to our images, patterns, textures, and designs—it allows them breathe and hopefully thrive.

The Japanese concept of Ma is concerned with leaving a gap or pause between two structural elements. It is an awareness of space that places an emphasis on the most important features of a form by paying attention to the shape of the negative space. Have you ever visited a Zen garden? There are only a few large rocks in an expanse of fine pebbles, representing islands in the ocean. These rocks are chosen carefully for their form, and even the raking in the pebbles echoes their form. It is a very peaceful, beautiful place to be. We can bring the beauty of emptiness into our quilts in some simple, easy ways.

Negative space can be very effective in quilt making. Consider the different effects just one block can have when colors are inverted or when they are rearranged. There are literally thousands of different ways to arrange a simple log cabin quilt and each time it becomes something different, even though the individual pieces are put together in a similar fashion. Some have names like fields and furrows, sunshine and shadows, barn raising, courthouse steps, chimneys and cornerstones, housetops, and many more.

Think about your next quilting project. How can you give it more breathing room? You can easily achieve it by increasing sashing or borders, while paying attention to contrast. When you choose the fabrics that you might include, remember that negative space can also be enhanced by negative space can also be enhanced by using low-volume prints in the same palette around the patchwork so that the negative space is easily seen and the design can be appreciated. If there are too many places for your eye to go, the effect can be lost as you wander, looking for a place to pause and appreciate.

mirror nature

Use quilting techniques in negative space to emphasize your original design. Try mirroring the design of the quilt into the background. The shape is echoed in quilting around the design like ripples on the water or the stones below.

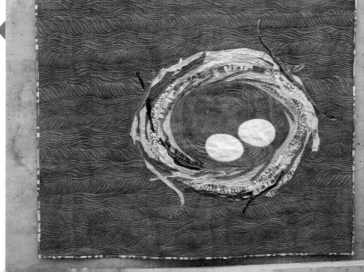

negative isn't always negative

Negative space can create a secondary pattern when you use solid fabric. Don't get stuck on white either. Gray, black, or even a muted color can be excellent background fabric. Or try reversing the background and the design, using solids for the pattern and prints for the background.

There's a place for breathing room, and there's a place for excess. So, don't get me wrong, there is nothing I love more than a spider web or crazy quilt design, but there is a time and place for everything. Sometimes we just need to infuse our work with a little air and light to let it shine. Most importantly, it isn't always what we put into a composition that makes it so powerful, but rather what we leave out.

all photos by Jill McNamara Photography used with permission from Carrie Bloomston

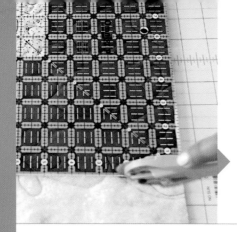

it's hip to be square

article by Edie McGinnis

After long hours of working so hard to piece your blocks, making sure all the points match up, you've got a finished quilt top on your hands and it's gorgeous! The corners are nearly perfect—I mean, you're a human, not a robot, right? And your quilt is all quilted, either by machine or by hand. But before you sew that binding on, there's one more step left. It's time to trim off the excess batting and backing, then you'll be ready to bind your quilt.

But before you begin trimming the edges, take a minute to think about this task. It might seem daunting but, by squaring up your beautiful quilt, you can change the comments on it from "how nice" to "wow!" Taking your quilt to the next level is all about preparation and attention to detail. Before you know it, you'll be able to tackle this task with confidence!

find a large, flat surface to work on
You can use your floor or a good-sized table. A dining room table with the leaves in place is just perfect. Don't move the chairs away from the table because they're like having a few extra hands around to help out. Quilts have a great deal of bulk to wrestle, but taming that mass of loveliness isn't as tough as you think. You can rest the bulk of the quilt over the backs of the chairs to keep the quilt from sliding everywhere.

gather your tools
You'll need a large square template (the bigger, the better for a large quilt), a long ruler that's at least 6" x 24", a rotary cutter, and your cutting mat. Throw in a large dose of patience while you're at it and you're ready to begin!

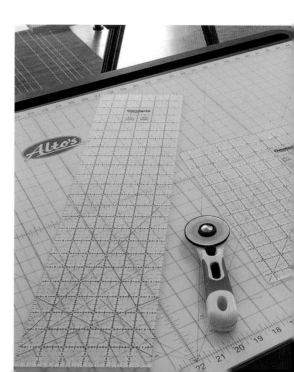

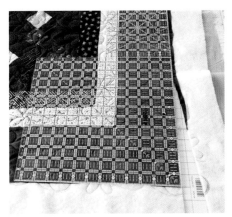

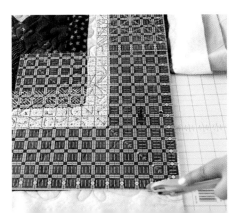

put your cutting mat in place

Keep in mind that a large mat won't slide around as much as a small one. No one needs the aggravation of trying to trim a large quilt while using a tiny mat that slips all over the place. You can even go the extra mile and use blue tape to secure it.

begin measuring in either of the lower corners of your quilt

If you are right handed, place the lower right corner of your quilt on the cutting mat. For lefties, begin working in the lower left corner. Smooth out your quilt so it lies flat. You don't want folds or wrinkles on the underside of the quilt to trip you up.

align your square ruler with the corner

Then place the long ruler up against the square and align the edge of that ruler with the edge of the quilt top. Because quilting tends to shrink and distort the top, you might notice places along the edge that don't line up exactly with the edge of the ruler. That's okay. You can gently pull the top to line up with those edges as you cut. If the edges are really wonky, you may have to trim off some of the quilt top along with the backing and batting. It's nothing to get too excited about because the point of squaring up a quilt is to make sure the edges are straight and the corners are at a 90-degree angle before you put on the binding. Just make sure all the borders are square and equal in width.

begin trimming the edges

Hold your ruler firmly in place as you cut. If you feel it start to slide, stop and realign the top and the rulers again. As you move up the edge, you will need to move your ruler as well. Each time, realign the ruler with the edge you have already cut, as well as with any available seam line.

keep the quilt top square as you round the next corner

Align your square ruler with the corner of the quilt like you did right at the beginning. Continue the process and line up the long ruler against the edge of the square and begin trimming again after you have turned the quilt so you are working from top to bottom.

continue trimming

Keep trimming until you have made it all the way around the quilt and all four sides are neat and tidy!

boxed weave
natalie earnheart

All quilters are all designers at heart, whether they acknowledge it or not. When I'm planning a quilt, I like to ask myself questions like "who am I making this quilt for?" "What style or taste does this person have?" "What is the purpose of this quilt?" For me, it is necessary to consider both the aesthetic and functional purposes of the quilt.

It amazes me to see all the variations that can be done with traditional quilt blocks. I'm often asked if I run out of ideas. Time yes, but ideas? No. By adding a sashing, setting the block on point, changing the size, or trying new colors, the design possibilities are endless. With quilting you can use color, shape, and texture to create works of art for daily use.

I love being a participant in the grand adventure that is quilting. I have fallen in love with the art and design as well as the process. I love how this quilt looks kind of like boxes of braids, or arrows pointing up in a new direction.

If I could offer quilters some advice, it would be to encourage them to go out and try something new today. Don't be afraid to head off in a different direction and make some mistakes. You never know what "happy accident" you'll come up with—it might become the best quilt you've ever made!

happy accidents!

It is important to think of the project as a process and do some research, testing, adjustment, and redesign. As quilters we are creative and artistic. We might make little mistakes and then, through the design process, turn them into new patterns. Some quilters I know call them "happy accidents."

perfection is overrated

Quilts aren't meant to be perfect. We stress over the little details when in reality, they're only visible to us! Don't worry too much about seams not matching up perfectly. A quilt should speak of it's origin and it was made by you.

▶ supply list

makes a 65" X 82" quilt

QUILT TOP
- 1 package 10" squares
- 3½ yards background fabric – includes inner border

BORDER
- 1¼ yards

BINDING
- ¾ yard

BACKING
- 5 yards

ADDITIONAL SUPPLIES
- 1 MSQC 10" Half Hexagon Template

SAMPLE QUILT
- **Cat Lady** by Sara Watts for Cotton+Steel

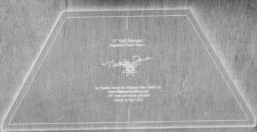

▶ *visit msqc.co/modblock2 for tutorials & info on how to make this quilt.*

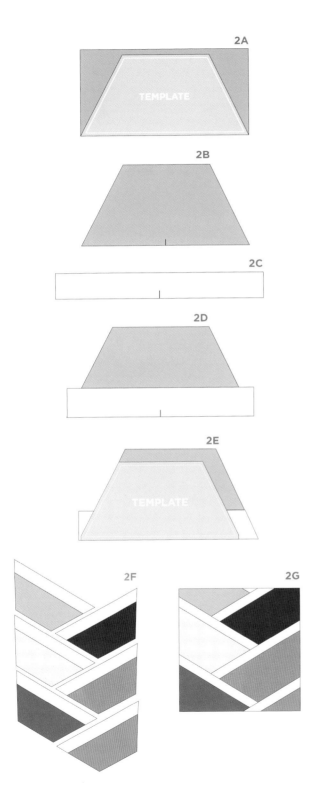

2A

2B

2C

2D

2E

2F

2G

1 cut

Select (36) 10″ squares from the package. Cut each in half, making 5″ x 10″ rectangles for a total of 72.

From the background fabric, cut:
- (72) 1½″ x 12″ sashing strips

2 trim

Place the Half Hexagon template on top of each of the 5″ x 10″ rectangles. Trim around the template. **2A**

Fold the half-hexagon pieces in half and press a crease (just use your fingers) at the halfway point on the widest edge. **2B**

Fold a 1½″ sashing strip in half and finger press a crease in place at the halfway point. **2C**

Match up the halfway point creases in the half-hexagon pieces and the sashing strip with right sides facing. Pin and sew the two pieces together. The sashing strip will extend past the edges of the hexagon piece. **2D**

After you have sewn the two pieces together, press the sashing away from the half-hexagon. Place the Half-Hexagon template back on the piece. Align the side edge of the template with the side of the print hexagon and the bottom of the white sashing strip and trim the white strip. Repeat for the other side of the half-hexagon. **Make 6** for each block, a **total of 72. 2E**

Sew the sashed half-hexagons together by following diagram. **2F Make 12.**

Trim the blocks to 12½″ square. **2G**

3 cut triangles & alternating blocks

From the background fabric, cut:
- (3) 18¼″ squares – cut the squares from corner to corner twice on the diagonal to make the side setting triangles. You will have two triangles left over.
- (2) 9⅜″ squares – cut the squares from corner to corner once on the diagonal to make the corner setting squares.
- (6) 12½″ squares – alternating blocks

4 layout quilt

Because the quilt is sewn together with the blocks on point, we will sew all the blocks together on the diagonal. Refer to the diagram on page 27 if necessary to see how each row goes together. **4A**

Beginning in the upper right hand corner, sew a setting triangle to two sides of one block to make the first row.

Row 2 begins with a setting triangle, followed by a pieced block. Add a white setting block, then a pieced block and end the row with a setting triangle.

1 Place the half-hexagon template on top of each of the 5" x 10" rectangles and trim around the template.

2 Add a 1½" sashing strip to the bottom of the piece.

3 Align the template with the side of the print hexagon and trim the strip.

4 Lay out the pieces in the order you want them sewn together.

5 Begin sewing the pieces together. Notice the first seam only goes across the short end of the block.

6 Trim and square the block to 12½".

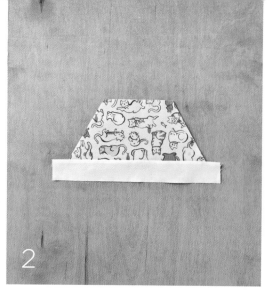

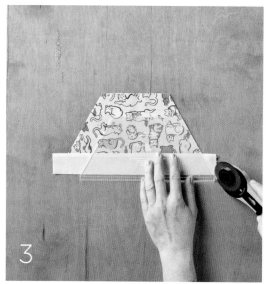

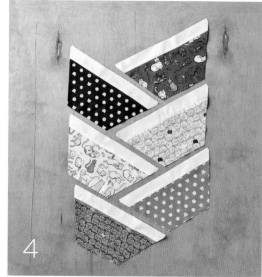

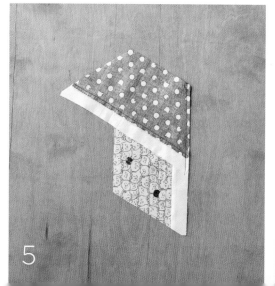

Row 3 begins with a corner triangle followed by a pieced block, then a white block, a pieced block, white block, a pieced block and finishes with a side setting triangle.

Row 4 begins with a side setting triangle and is followed by a pieced block, a white block, a pieced block, a white block, a pieced block and ends with a corner triangle.

Row 5 is a repeat of row 2.

Row 6 is a repeat of row 1. Sew all the rows together. Add a corner triangle to the upper right corner and the lower left corner to complete the center of the quilt.

5 inner border

Cut (7) 2½″ strips across the width of the fabric. Sew the strips together end-to-end to make one long strip. Trim the borders from this strip.

Refer to Borders (pg. 103) in the Construction Basics to measure and cut the outer borders. The strips are approximately 68½″ for the sides and approximately 55½″ for the top and bottom.

6 outer border

Cut (7) 5½″ strips across the width of the fabric. Sew the strips together end-to-end to make one

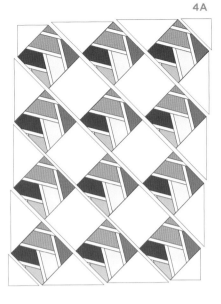

long strip. Trim the borders from this strip.

Refer to Borders (pg. 103) in the Construction Basics to measure and cut the outer borders. The strips are approximately 72½″ for the sides and approximately 65½″ for the top and bottom. **7A**

7 quilt and bind

Layer the quilt with batting and backing and quilt. After the quilting is complete, square up the quilt and trim away all excess batting and backing. Add binding to complete the quilt. See Construction Basics (pg. 104) for binding instructions. **7A**

cornerstone
amy ellis

Quilting is full of possibilities. A set of blocks can form an entirely new pattern by simply rotating them or laying them out in a different way. It turns an expected design into a hidden surprise! The interaction between quilt blocks is one of my favorite things about quilting.

For the "Cornerstone" quilt, I have taken two different half-square triangle groups and put them together. I love the secondary design element that pops up! There are many complex quilts out there, but quilts like this—that are simple to make, yet intricate at first glance—are always at the top of my list!

Making "Cornerstone" was a lot of fun and relatively simple. Usually I like all the half-square triangles in a pattern to be the same size, but in this case, it worked to my advantage that half of them were larger than the rest. The finished effect of this quilt makes it seem a lot more complicated than it was to put together. All the half-square triangles work together, coming alive against the white background, full of energy and motion. Give your half-square triangles new life by changing up the size and placement. You'll love the results!

half-square, half the work

Making "Cornerstone" was a lot of fun and relatively simple. Usually I like all the half-square triangles in a pattern to be the same size, but in this case, it worked to my advantage that half of them were larger than the rest.

the breakdown

When you break this pattern down, it's essentially a maple leaf block (with no stem) and another block made up of four half-square triangles, broken up by white sashing with patterned corner squares. So, when you divide the quilt up, one block has four triangles and one has six, but it's totally okay! This means that you don't have to match up the points when sewing the sections together—which is a big help when you're sewing together so many triangles!

▸ supply list

makes a 74" X 88" quilt

QUILT TOP
- 15 fat quarters
- 5 yards eggshell (Moda Bella solid 281)

BACKING
- 5¼ yards

BINDING
- ⅔ yard

SAMPLE QUILT
- **Serenity** by Amy Ellis for Moda Fabrics
- **Bella Solids Eggshell** (281) by Moda Fabrics

▸ *visit msqc.co/modblock2 for tutorials & info on how to make this quilt.*

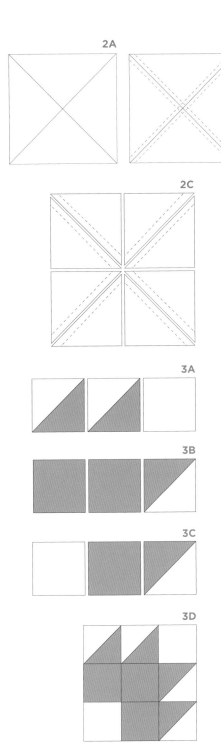

1 cut

From each fat quarter, cut:
- (2) 8" squares
- (2) 6" squares
- (14) 2½" squares

From the eggshell, cut:
- (6) 8" x WOF strips – Subcut the strips into (30) 8" squares.
- (5) 6" x WOF strips – Subcut into (30) 6" squares.
- (8) 6½" x WOF strips – Subcut into (120) 2½" x 6½" rectangles.
- (8) 2½" x WOF strips - Subcut into (120) 2½" squares.

2 block construction

Draw a line from corner to corner twice on the diagonal on the reverse side of the 6" and 8" solid eggshell squares. **2A**

Layer an eggshell square with a print square of the same size with right sides facing, and sew ¼" on either side of the marked lines. **2B**

Cut through the center of the sewn squares vertically and horizontally then cut along the drawn lines. Each square set yields **8 half-square triangle units. 2C**

Trim the larger half-square triangles to 3½" and the smaller ones to 2½". Open each and press the seam allowance toward the print fabric.

3 block A

Sew (2) 2½" half-square triangles to (1) 2½" eggshell square as shown. **3A**

Sew (2) 2½" print squares to a 2½" half-square triangle. **3B**

Sew 1 eggshell 2½" square to a print 2½" square. Add a half-square triangle. **3C**

Sew the three rows together to make a corner unit. **Make 4** for each block. **3D**

Sew a corner unit to either side of an eggshell 2½" x 6½" rectangle. **Make 2** and press the seam allowances toward the corner units. **3E**

Sew an eggshell 2½" rectangle to either side of a print 2½" square.

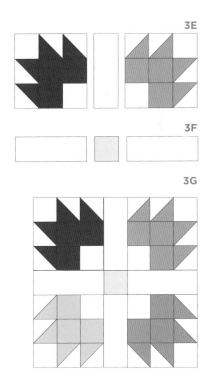

1 Draw a line from corner to corner twice on the diagonal. Sew ¼" on either side of the line. Cut through the center vertically and horizontally, then on the drawn lines to make 8 half-square triangles.

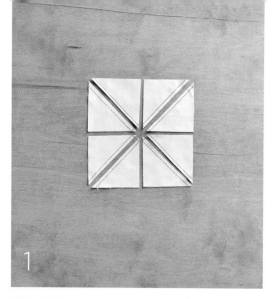

2 Make a corner unit for Block A by sewing half-square triangles and squares together as shown.

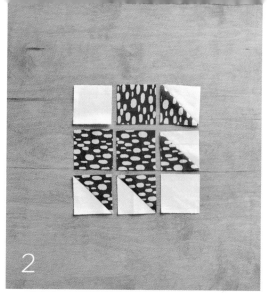

3 Sew the units for Block A together as shown to complete the block.

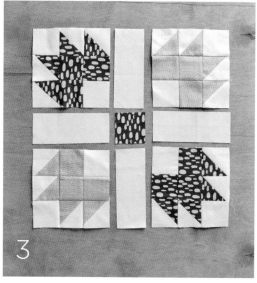

4 Sew 4 half-square triangles together to make a corner unit for block B.

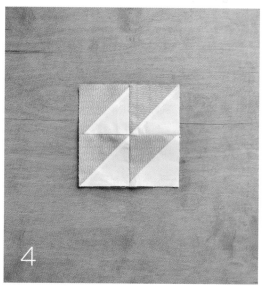

5 Sew the units for Block B together in rows as shown.

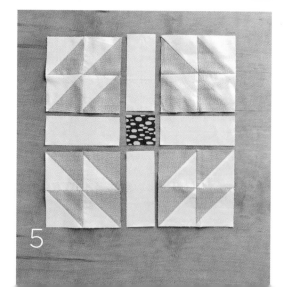

Press the seam allowances toward the print square. **3F**

Sew the **three rows** together to complete 1 Block A. **Make 15**. **3G**

4 block B

Sew (4) 3½" half-square triangles together as shown to make a corner unit. **Make 4** for each block. **4A**

Sew a corner unit to either side of an eggshell 2½" x 6½" rectangle.

Make 2 and press the seam allowances toward the corner unit. **4B**

Sew an eggshell 2½" rectangle to either side of a print 2½" square. Press the seam allowances toward the print square. **4C**

Sew the **three rows** together to complete 1 Block B. **Make 15. 4D**

5 quilt construction

Lay out **six rows** of **five blocks** each, alternating the A and B blocks as shown in the diagram on the upper right. Also, note the nesting of seams and turn the blocks as needed.

Pin and sew the blocks together, row-by-row, pressing the seam allowances toward block B. Pin and sew the rows together, pressing the seam allowances in one direction.

6 borders

From the eggshell fabric, cut (8) 2½" x 42" strips. Sew the strips end-to-end to make one long strip.

4A

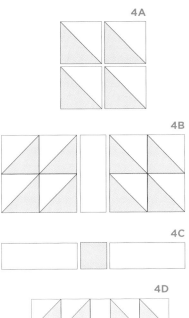

4B

4C

4D

Cut the borders from this strip. Refer to Borders (pg. 103) in the Construction Basics to measure and cut the outer borders. The strips are approximately 84½" for the sides and approximately 74½" for the top and bottom.

7 quilt and bind

Layer the quilt with batting and backing and quilt. After the quilting is complete, square up the quilt and trim away all excess batting and backing. Add binding to complete the quilt. See Construction Basics (pg. 104) for binding instructions.

moonlight
victoria findlay wolfe

Have you opened up one of those coloring books for adults recently? Unlike a child's coloring book, the geometric or nature-inspired patterns are complex and inspiring, just begging to be filled in with bold strokes of color.

As a modern quilter, I like to look at traditional quilt patterns in the same way, breaking them down into black and white line drawings, and then choosing which colors or patterns I'm going to use to fill in that design. It's a very useful exercise to see patterns with a fresh pair of eyes.

The first and obvious design of a quilt is only the start of finding many more options. When you look at the shape of the quilt blocks, you get to be the artist and decide which colors you are going to use to fill in those shapes. Try breaking the pattern down into the individual pieces of the block, sashing, and border and think about the alternate designs that could emerge.

Think, "How can I make this modern?" "Am I using my negative space as a potential secondary pattern?"

Keeping that thought in mind about negative space, I keep telling the story of the quilt all the way out to the binding. I chose to bind the quilt in the same rich blue, to further enhance the ethereal evening star feel. If you wanted to pull in tiny bits of orange into your binding in various spots, that too would be a great way to enhance the "twinkle" effect! I'll leave that up to you. Go forth and dissect your quilt patterns! Exciting designs are lurking in even the most unlikely quilts. Have fun playing with color and looking at patterns with new eyes!

▶ the sashing effect

Take note! Not all the sashing is the same in this quilt! By highlighting only some of the sashing in the two main "stars," I created more negative space. Also, by adding the darker orange in the "cornerstones" of the sashing, and keeping the blue background around the blocks, it gave the entire quilt the illusion that the blocks are floating in a deep cobalt "sky."

break it down

You can have so much fun exploring color placement when you make your own unique design. In this quilt, I started with a "Cedars of Lebanon" block. By breaking down this traditional block into a two color palette of hot pink and blue, it became an interplay of positive and negative space. Simplifying the color palette helped bring out an entirely new design.

▸ supply list

makes a 68" X 82" quilt

QUILT TOP
- 5½ yards Pacific Blue (K001-90) – includes border and binding
- ¾ yard Honeysuckle (K001-490)
- ½ yard Peach (K001-1281)
- ¼ yard Torch (K001-450)

BACKING
- 4¼ yards Honeysuckle (K001-490)

SAMPLE QUILT
- **Kona Solids** by Robert Kaufman

▸ *visit msqc.co/modblock2 for tutorials & info on how to make this quilt.*

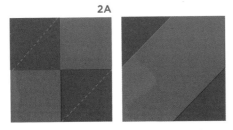

2A

2B

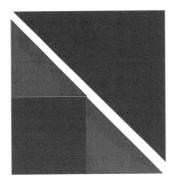

2C

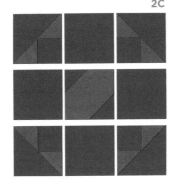

1 cut

From Pacific Blue, cut:
- (72) 2½" squares
- (24) 4⅞" squares, cut each in half once on the diagonal to make 2 triangles, for a **total of 48.**
- (48) 4½" squares
- (23) 2½" x 12½" strips for sashing
- (2) 12½" x 44½" for top and bottom borders
- (2) 12½" x 82½" for left and right side borders (cut (4) 12½" strips across the width of the fabric, trim off selvages and sew 2 strips together along the short ends. Trim to 82½" long.)

From Hot Pink, cut:
- (12) 4½" squares
- (48) 2⅞" squares, cut each in half once on the diagonal to make 2 triangles, for a **total of 96.**

From Peach, cut:
- (8) 2½" x 12½" strips for sashing

From Torch, cut:
- (20) 2½" squares for cornerstones

2 block construction

Unit A: On the back of 2 of the Pacific Blue 2½" squares, draw a line from corner to corner once on the diagonal. Place one on a hot pink 4½" square, with right sides facing, aligning the edges of one corner. Sew on the diagonal line. Trim the excess fabric ¼" away from the seam line. Flip open and press. Repeat with the other blue square on the opposite corner of the same pink square. **2A**

Unit B: Sew 2 hot pink triangles to a blue 2½" square as shown. Then sew a blue half-square triangle to the long edge, forming a square. **Make 4** of these units. **2B**

Sew a Unit B to either side of a blue 4½" square. Make **2 rows** like this. Then sew a blue 4½" square to either side of a Unit A. Make **1 row.** Sew the **3 rows** together as shown, pressing the seams toward the solid blue squares. This will result in the seams going in opposite directions and "nesting" together as you pin and sew the rows together. **2C**

Make 12 blocks.

3 quilt construction

Arrange the blocks as shown. Make sure the blocks are angled in the correct direction!

1 Sew a 2½" blue square to either side of a 4½" pink squares. Trim the excess fabric ¼" from the sewn seams.

2 After trimming, open the center unit and press.

3 Sew a hot pink triangle to either side of a blue 2½" square as shown.

4 Complete Unit B by adding a blue half-square triangle to the long edge.

5 Sew the block together in rows as shown.

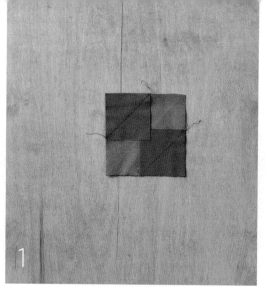
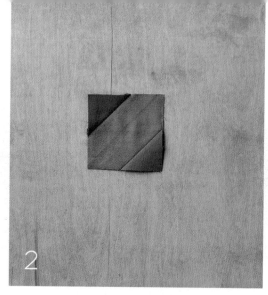
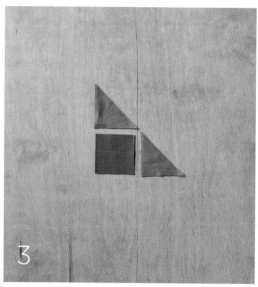
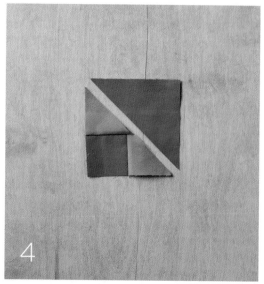
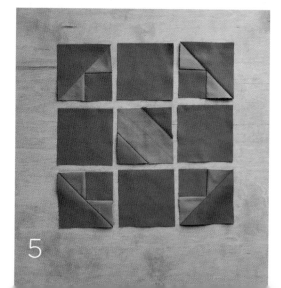

3A

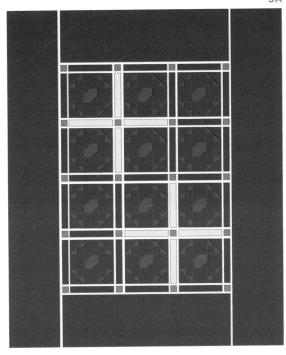

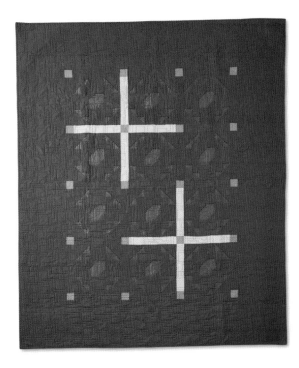

Starting in the upper left corner of the quilt, sew the left side sashing to the block. Then sew the upper left cornerstone to the top sashing strip and sew to the top of the block.

Continue in this manner, sewing the left and top sashings with cornerstones to each block. When you reach the blocks on the right and bottom edges of the quilt, add the remaining sashing strips and cornerstones to those blocks. Sew the blocks together, pinning at the intersections. **3A**

Find the center of the top edge of the quilt by folding it in half, finger pressing and placing a pin to mark. Do the same on one of the shorter border pieces. Match the ends and centers together, pin and sew on the top border. Sew on bottom border in the same way. Press. Repeat for the two side borders.

4 quilt and bind

Layer the quilt with batting and backing and quilt. After the quilting is complete, square up the quilt and trim away all excess batting and backing. Add binding to complete the quilt. See Construction Basics (page 104) for binding instructions.

rhombus dance
christine ricks

Have you ever come across a tiled floor with an intriguing design and thought to yourself "that would make a great quilt?" This happens to me almost daily.

While I'm out enjoying nature or just walking down the street, I often stop to take pictures of patterns that inspire me. That's actually how the Rhombus Dance quilt came about. I had seen a similar tile pattern during one of my travels and became obsessed with it. In the quilting world, it's often referred to as "tumbling blocks."

This rhombille pattern can be found in ancient Greek mosaics and ceilings in cathedrals. There's something special about the way it plays tricks on your eyes. This pattern eludes many quilters because of it's complex piecing arrangement, full of Y seams that require paper piecing. I had shied away from the pattern for years, but I knew the time had come to tackle it, so I had the idea of designing a tool that would help make it easier to sew in rows instead of blocks. That was the key! With a little help from the MSQC team we made it happen and the Rhombus Dance quilt became a reality.

By looking at this pattern in a different way, I was able to simplify the construction using the new rhombus tool that I designed. When you look at a rhombus, it's really just two equilateral triangles put together, so I thought, "Why not leave some whole and, when necessary, add a triangle to complete the design? If the colors match up, it achieves the same effect as the more complex Y seam piecing." Ta da! Because of this simple trick, form and function came together to make this really fun and easy quilt.

▶ eyes wide open

Keep your eyes open to inspiration whereever you are. Whether you're standing in line at the grocery store or traveling to exotic places, design is everywhere. You might be surprised where you find it if you keep yourself open to it.

playing with the shapes ◀

This rhombus shape lends itself to so many options. Try different color combinations to create different designs. You can make arrows, chevrons, or even a star shape. Have fun creating your own unique layout!

▸ supply list

makes a 52" X 65" quilt

QUILT TOP
RJR Cotton Supreme Solids
• ½ yard Elephantastic Pink (RJR-9617-277)
• ¼ yard Paris (RJR-9617-235 RP)
• ½ yard Tickled Pink (RJR-9617-330)
• ½ yard Tiffany Box (RJR-9617-291)
• 1¼ yards Bayou (RJR-9617-344)
• ½ yard Navy (RJR-9617-30T)
• 2½ yards On The Rocks (RJR-9617-283)

BACKING
• 3½ yards

BINDING
• ¾ yard

TOOLS
• MSQC Rhombus Template

SAMPLE QUILT
• RJR Cotton Supreme Solids

▸ *visit msqc.co/modblock2 for tutorials*
& info on how to make this quilt.

1 cut

Use the Rhombus template to cut all rhombuses as well as the required number of triangles.

From the light peach, cut:
- (3) 5" strips across the width of the fabric – subcut the strips into 14 rhombuses and 2 triangles.

From the medium peach, cut:
- (1) 5" strip across the width of the fabric – subcut the strip into 8 triangles.

From the pink, cut:
- (2) 5" strips across the width of the fabric – subcut the strips into 1 rhombus and 10 triangles.

From the turquoise, cut:
- (2) 5" strips across the width of the fabric – subcut the strips into 12 triangles.

From the dark green, cut:
- (1) 5" strip across the width of the fabric – subcut into 5 rhombuses.

From the navy blue, cut:
- (2) 5" strips – subcut the strips into 10 rhombuses.

From the gray fabric, cut:
- (3) 10 ½" strips across the width of the fabric.

- (11) 5" strips across the width of the fabric – subcut 5 strips into 17 rhombuses and 16 triangles.
  - Subcut 1 strip into (3) 13" lengths.
  - Subcut each of 2 of the strips into (1) 11" and (1) 23" lengths.

The 2 remaining strips will be trimmed to size after the quilt is sewn together.

Before you begin to sew, lay out each row according to the diagrams provided.

2 sew in rows

Row 1: Trim a gray strip with the rhombus template with the angle on the end going from lower right to upper left. Refer to diagram **2A** and stitch the rhombuses and triangles together as shown. Add the gray strip last.

2A

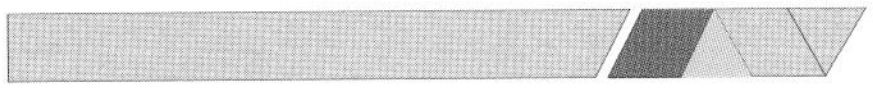

Row 2: Trim a strip with the rhombus template with the angle on the end going from lower right to upper left. Refer to diagram **2B** and sew the rhombuses and triangles together as shown. Add the gray strip last.

2B

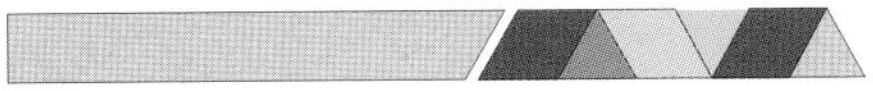

▶ **NOTE** *After the rows are sewn together, the quilt will be trimmed and squared, you can expect the rows to be uneven. But as long as the rhombuses and triangles are aligned as shown in the diagrams, everything will come out fine. We will be adding the large top and bottom strips last.*

Row 3: Trim a 13" gray strip using the rhombus template with the angle going from lower right to upper left. Refer to diagram **2C** and sew the rhombuses and triangles together as shown. Add the 13" strip last.

2C

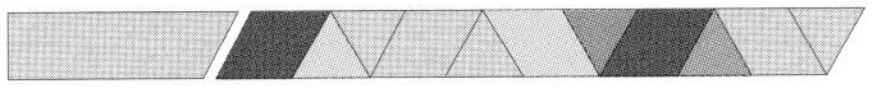

Row 4: Refer to diagram **2D** and sew the rhombuses and triangles together as shown. Add a 13" gray strip trimmed at the correct angle (lower right to upper left).

2D

Row 5: Refer to diagram **2E** and stitch the rhombuses and triangles together as shown. Add a 13" gray strip to the right after trimming the proper angle. Add an 11" strip to the left side of the strip after trimming it at the angle shown.

2E

Row 6: Refer to diagram **2F** and sew the rhombuses and the triangles together as shown. Complete the row by adding an 11″ strip after trimming it at the proper angle.

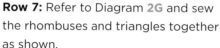

2F

Row 7: Refer to Diagram **2G** and sew the rhombuses and triangles together as shown.

2G

Row 8: Refer to Diagram **2H** and sew the rhombuses and triangles together as shown.

2H

Row 9: Refer to Diagram **2I** and sew the rhombuses and the triangles together as shown. Trim a 22″ strip at the angle shown and sew it to the turquoise triangle.

2I

Row 10: Refer to Diagram **2J** and sew the triangles and rhombuses together as shown. Trim a 22″ strip on the angle as shown and stitch it to the turquoise triangle.

2J

3 sew rows together

Sew rows 1 through 10 together. Align a large square rotary cutting ruler (the bigger the better!) along the bottom edge of the quilt top in

1   Cut a 5″ strip. Place the rhombus template on the strip and cut the required number of shapes needed.

2   To cut triangles using the rhombus template, align the etched line with the bottom of the strip. Cut the required number of triangles needed.

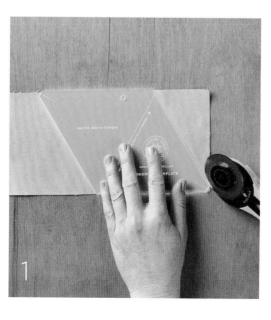

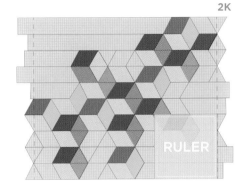

2K

one corner. Because your rows finish at 4½", you should be able to align ruler marks along the seam lines as well to make sure you are able to trim the edges straight. Using your rotary cutter, trim the edge. When you reach the end of the ruler, scoot it up and make sure all your marks are aligned and continue to trim until you reach the top of the quilt. Repeat for the other side. **2K**

Sew the (3) 10½" strips together. Cut the pieces for the top and bottom of the quilt from this strip. Measure the quilt from side to side. Make 2 strips this measurement (approximately 52½"). Sew one to the top and one to the bottom of the quilt.

4 quilt and bind

Layer the quilt with batting and backing and quilt. After the quilting is complete, square up the quilt and trim away all excess batting and backing. Add binding to complete the quilt. See Construction Basics (pg. 104) for binding instructions.

light box
christopher thompson

On a random weekend in October I found myself experiencing the works of Dan Flavin for the first time. He was being featured at one of the many art galleries in Chelsea and I happened upon his exhibit. It left a deep impression on me.

He was an artist from New York, who died way too young. No stranger to the world of art, Mr. Flavin began his career with sketches inspired by abstract expressionism. His later work includes sketches for sculptures that feature electric lights and awe-inspiring neon light installations. Much like quilting, these sculptures explore color, light, and negative space.

Dan Flavin's light sculptures inspired the "Light Box" quilt, using one color against a black and white background, emulating light and shadow. In the dazzling world of quilting, paring down your color choices can be a difficult task! Try picking just one color for a monochromatic effect, or even using only black and white. This allows the pattern to become the focus, instead of the interplay of the patterned fabric—which is another fun approach to quilting—but in this case, minimalism is key.

For me, art and quilting have always gone hand in hand. One of the earliest forms of art in America was quilting, a tradition that lives on strong today. The form and function of quilting has evolved into many different variations beyond the traditional. In that way, it shifts and changes to fit our lives and express our individual perspectives. It's fun to see how each person is inspired by the world around them! What inspires you? Now go turn your artistic vision into a quilt!

53

creative processes

I don't know that I have a specific creative process. I love exploring. I feel like my best quilts are the quilts that had a background story to them. If I'm given a challenge, I let the fabric do the talking. I love to look at the fabric, mixing and matching it until the balance of color and print is just right.

stand out from the crowd

I once heard that when you throw a party, you need that one loud friend. I believe that's true with pulling fabrics, you need that one loud, standout print or color.

shifting form ◀

Modern quilts explore color, light, and negative space. Color and negative space are totally up to the maker, but light is natural and can transform a design, so look at your quilt in daylight. Shadows play tricks, colors appear brighter and bolder at times, even a freshly washed quilt is transformative. The function is still there, but the shape has been transformed.

▸ supply list

makes a 44" X 40½" quilt

QUILT TOP
- ¼ yard Azalea (Moda Bella solid 9900 144)
- 1 yard White (Moda Bella solid 9900 98)
- 1½ yard Black (Moda Bella solid 9900 99) - includes binding

BACKING
- 1½ yards

SAMPLE QUILT
- **Bella Solids** by Moda Fabric

▸ *visit msqc.co/modblock2 for tutorials & info on how to make this quilt.*

1 cut

From the pink fabric, cut:
- (3) 2½" x 19¼" strips

From the white fabric, cut:
- (8) 2½" x 41" strips
- (3) 2½" x 19¼" strips

From the black fabric, cut:
- (8) 2½" x 41" strips
- (6) 2½" x 12½" strips
- (6) 2½" x 10¼" strips

2 sew unit A

Sew a black 2½" x 10¼" strip to one end of a white 2½" x 19¼" strip. Add a black 2½" x 12½" strip to the opposite end of the white strip. **Make 3. 2A**

3 sew unit B

Sew a black 2½" x 10¼" strip to one end of a white 2½" x 19¼" strip. Add a black 2½" x 12½" strip to the opposite end of the white strip. **Make 3. 3A**

4 quilt construction

Refer to diagram 4A and sew the strips together to complete the quilt top. As you sew the strips together, press toward the darker color. **4A**

5 quilt and bind

Layer the quilt top with backing and batting and quilt as you please. Square up the quilt and add binding to finish. We cut the binding for this quilt 2¼" wide. See the Construction Basics on page 104 for binding instructions.

2A

3A

▶ **TIP** *Instead of a pink, try a colorful print or sew several 2½" squares together for a scrappy look.*

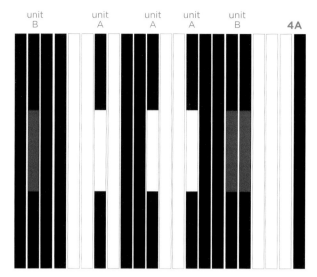

tiny wonky star
jenny doan

Life is so full of possibilities at that moment right after high school, leading into the college years. I remember it was at about that age that I met my husband. My granddaughter Annie is right at that precious time in her life and headed off to college. We hate to see her go, but we know wonderful things are in store for her.

I wanted to make Annie a quilt to help her keep her family close while she's away. I chose a Wonky Star pattern because my granddaughter has a strong personality and is definitely okay with who she is, so these stars remind me of her. It's alright to be a little wonky! Each star is different and beautiful in its own way. I loved putting them together and each time I finished a block I would gaze at it, admiring how unique each one was. It made me feel like an abstract artist as I experimented with color and design.

Using my imagination is one of the things I love most about quilting. If we gave ten quilters the same bundle of fabric, they would each make something different with it. I love seeing the all the many ways people use fabric and patterns. The Wonky Star quilt is the perfect example of this because it gives you the opportunity to play with colors you choose and you get to decide the length of each point on the star—some might be longer, some shorter, some thicker, and some thinner. The great part is, when it all comes together, it looks fantastic!

I know that I tend to create in an area I am comfortable in and maybe that's true for most of us, but it's never too late to try something new. Always be grateful for your imagination and don't be afraid to let your wonky star shine!

hop on board the imagination train

Using my imagination is one of the things I love most about quilting. If we gave ten quilters the same bundle of fabric, they would each make something different with it. I love seeing the all the many ways people use fabric and patterns. The Wonky Star quilt is the perfect example of this because it gives you the opportunity to play with colors you choose and you get to decide the length of each point on the star—some might be longer, some shorter, some thicker, and some thinner. The great part is, when it all comes together, it looks fantastic!

starry, starry night

Think of how cool it would be to invert the white background on this quilt and make it darker, perhaps a deep navy blue or even black. The stars could be made from lighter colored fabric to create greater contrast. Against this dark canvas, they would shine like stars in the sky at night.

▶ supply list

makes a 69" X 81" quilt

QUILT TOP
• 1 roll of 2½" print strips
• 5¼ yards background fabric –
  includes borders

BACKING
• 5 yards

BINDING
• ¾ yard

SAMPLE QUILT
• **Essential Magic Colors** by
  Wilmington Prints
• **Bella Solids Bleached White**
  (9900 98)

▶ *visit msqc.co/modblock2 for tutorials*
& info on how to make this quilt.

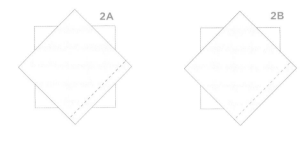

1 cut

From the background fabric, cut:
- (60) 6½" squares
- (480) 2½" squares

From the 2½" print strips, cut:
- (180) 2½" squares –
set aside 60 for the center
of each block

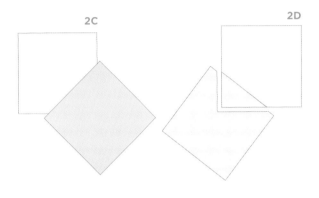

2 sew star points

Place a 2½" print square on
an angle (any angle) atop a
background 2½" square with right
sides facing. Make sure your print
square is placed a little past the
halfway point. Sew ¼" in from the
angled edge of the print square.
Trim ¼" away from the sewn seam.
2A 2B

Press the piece flat then turn the
square over and press the print
piece over the seam allowance.
Trim the print so all edges are even
with the background square. Set
the trimmed print scrap aside
to use for another leg of the star.
(You should be able to make at
least two star legs from each print
square.) **2C 2D**

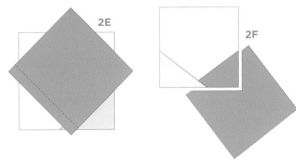

Place another 2½" print square on
the adjacent side of the square.
Make sure the edge of the second
print crosses over the first print by
at least ¼". Stitch ¼" in from the
edge of the print. Trim the excess
away ¼" from the sewn seam. **2E**
Press the print piece over the seam
allowance. Turn the square over
and trim so all edges are even.
Notice your square is still 2½".
Make 4. 2F 2G

3 put block together

Sew a background square to either
side of a star point square. **Make
two rows** like this. **3A**

▶ **NOTE** *Have fun with this
and don't try to make all the
points alike!*

Sew a star point to either side of
a print square. Make sure the star
points face away from the center
square. **3B**

Sew the three rows together as
shown to complete the block.
Make 60. 3C

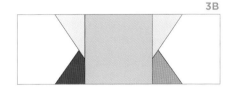

1 Sew a 2½" square to a background square at an angle. Any angle will do as long as the piece goes a little over the halfway point of the background square.

2 Trim ¼" away from the sewn seam and square up the block.

3 Sew another 2½" print square to the adjacent side of the square.

4 Trim ¼" away from the sewn seam, press and trim the edges to match the background square.

5 Sew a 2½" background square to either side of a star point.

6 Sew the star units together into rows as shown.

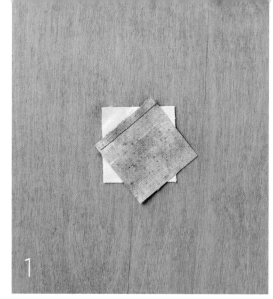

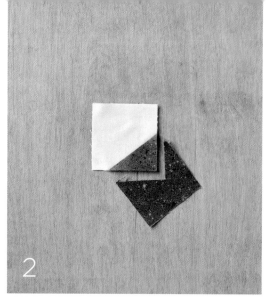

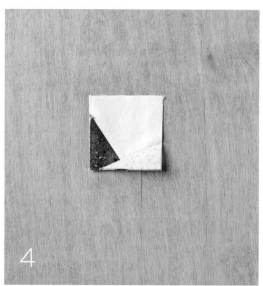

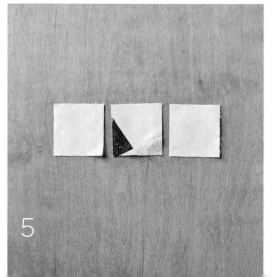

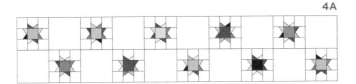

4 lay out the rows

Arrange the blocks in **rows of 10**. Each row has **5 star blocks** and **5 setting squares** that alternate. **Make 12 rows**. 4A

Press the seam allowances of the odd numbered rows toward the left and even numbered rows toward the right. Sew the rows together.

5 border

Cut (8) 5″ strips across the width of the fabric. Sew the strips together end-to-end to make one long strip. Trim the borders from this strip. Refer to Borders page 103 in the Construction Basics to measure and cut the borders. The strips are approximately 72½″ for the sides and approximately 69½″ for the top and bottom.

6 quilt and bind

Layer the quilt with batting and backing and quilt. After the quilting is complete, square up the quilt and trim away all excess batting and backing. Add binding to complete the quilt. See Construction Basics page 104 for binding instructions.

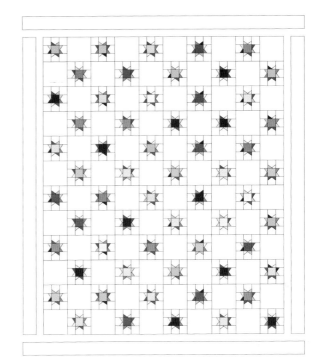

rising star
ron doan

To my mother's chagrin, taking jumps was one of my favorite things to do on my motorcycle. The feeling of flying off jumps was such a thrill! I raced for many years and to this day, I still love to ride. In addition to riding my motorcycle, I now quilt—I had to keep up with my wife! For my most recent quilt, I wanted to try out a new pattern and play with variations of it to see what design might appear.

I made this Rising Star quilt with the idea that it's designed for versatility. As I was working on it alongside Jenny, We realized as we rotated the block, trying different settings, that in one variation, it became a four-pointed star. Because of that discovery we decided to call it "Rising Star." We chose these fabrics because we thought the gray background worked well with the edgy designs in Carolyn Friedlander's Carkai fabric collection. I often finish quilts on my own, but this time we used MSQC's fabulous machine quilting services to do the job. The flame-inspired stitch just seemed to work with such a unique pattern.

Even though I still love riding, I am proud to say that I now love quilting as well—maybe not as much as Jenny does—but it's still a lot of fun. The bonus is that when I quilt, I get to spend time with my wife too. Quilting keeps my creative juices flowing and nowadays it's a lot easier on the bones than jumping motorcycles!

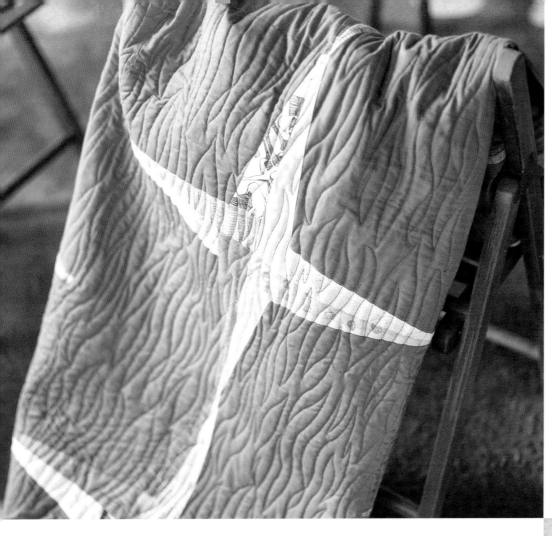

rotate and reveal

This quilt makes a beautiful star, but think of what else might happen with this pattern if just one of the sections were rotated? Keep on experimenting and you'll be surprised at what you'll come up with!

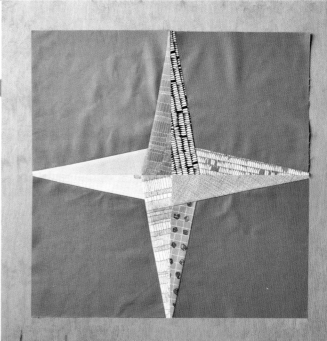

▶ supply list

Makes a 57" X 66½" quilt

QUILT TOP
- 1 roll of 2½" strips
- 1 package of 10" squares
  (42 count)

BACKING
- 3¾ yards

BINDING
- ¾ yard

SAMPLE QUILT
- **Carkai** by Carolyn Friedlander
  for Robert Kauffman
- **Kona Cotton Steel** Yardage
  by Robert Kaufman for Robert
  Kaufman

▶ *visit msqc.co/modblock2 for tutorials*
& info on how to make this quilt.

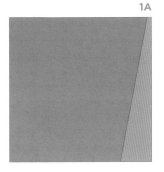

1A

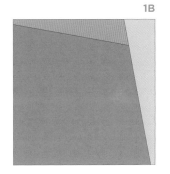

1B

2A

1 sew and trim

Place a 2½" strip on one edge of a 10" square. Make sure the strip extends past the edge of the square. Stitch in place sewing at an angle. Trim the ends and the side of the strip even with the square. Trim any excess fabric away ¼" from the seam line. Press. **1A** Repeat using a different colored 2½" strip on the adjacent corner of the 10" square. **Make 42 blocks. 2A**

2 arrange in rows

Arrange the blocks in **7 rows** with each row consisting of **6 blocks.** Refer to diagram **2A** when arranging the blocks if you would like your quilt to have the same layout.

3 quilt and bind

Layer the quilt with batting and backing and quilt. After the quilting is complete, square up the quilt and trim away all excess batting and backing. Add binding to complete the quilt. See Construction Basics (page 104) for binding instructions.

1   Sew a 2½" strip to a 10" gray square on an angle making sure that when you flip the strip over, the space will be covered.

2   Trim the strip even with the square.

3   Add another strip to the adjacent corner of the square.

4   Trim the strip so it is even with the square.

5   Sew the blocks together into rows. As the rows are completed, you will see the stars emerge.

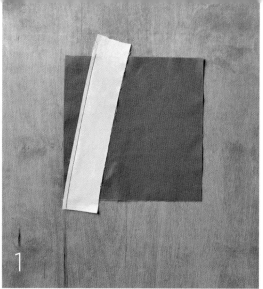

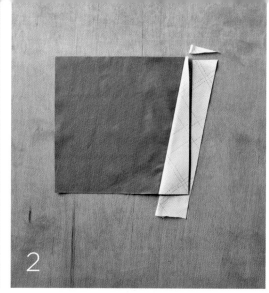

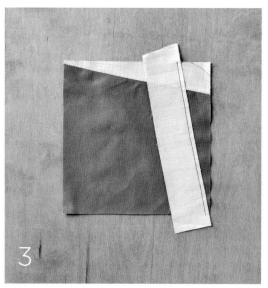

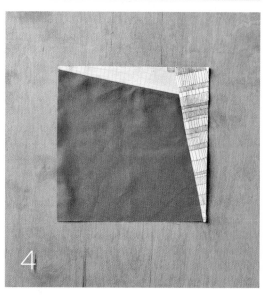

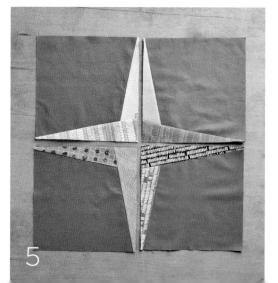

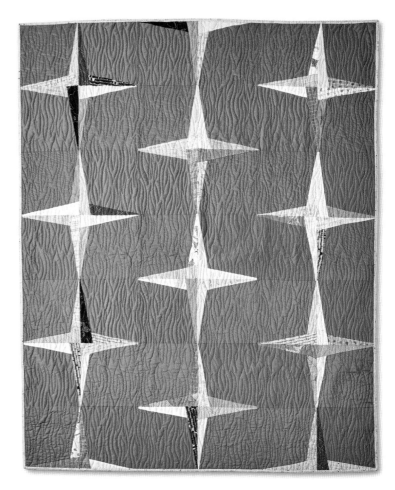

▶slice-a-block
rob appell

Modern quilting has opened up so many possibilities in design and construction with simple changes to traditional designs. Giving quilts more negative space allows for more quilting options. These vast fabric expanses beautifully showcase great free-motion machine quilting. In this quilt, there is plenty of space to play with unique quilting designs.

I also love the freedom that comes with creating quilts that offer easy to piece blocks as well as the design-as-you-go feel. Building the exact same block can become a bit tedious and time consuming, so I started playing with the concept of simply adding a strip in each block with no particular layout in mind. I discovered that the Slice-a-Block is a ridiculously fast and fun quilt to make!

I fell in love with Grunge from Moda, and, of course, Robert Kaufman's pre-cut skinny 1½″ black strips made this project a snap. You can slice the block in any place you'd like and add in the black strip. Try laying out the blocks so that the black strips go in many different directions for variety. Give it a try, there's no wrong way to make this quilt and you'll love the results time and time again!

► **go grunge or go home**

Get out your old Dr. Martens and plaid flannel shirt from the back of your closet. Grunge is back and it's going to rock your world! I'm talking about Grunge fabric by Basicgrey for Moda. These distressed hues look worn but feel brand new. They're perfect for this project. It's an exploration of color and texture broken up by black diagonal lines. It's an easy way to take basic patchwork to the next level.

SUNSHINE
FEEDS THE
SOUL

slice and dice ◄

In this project, one diagonal line was used to break up the block, but what about two? The effect would be very cool! Keep on slicing and dicing. You'll have a lot of fun experimenting.

▶ supply list

makes a 56" X 65" quilt

QUILT TOP
• 1 package of 10" squares
  (42 count)
• (1) 1½" roll Black strips

BACKING & BINDING
• 4 yards Kona Black

SAMPLE QUILT
• **Grunge** by Moda Fabrics
• **Bella Solids Black**

▶ *visit msqc.co/modblock2 for tutorials
& info on how to make this quilt.*

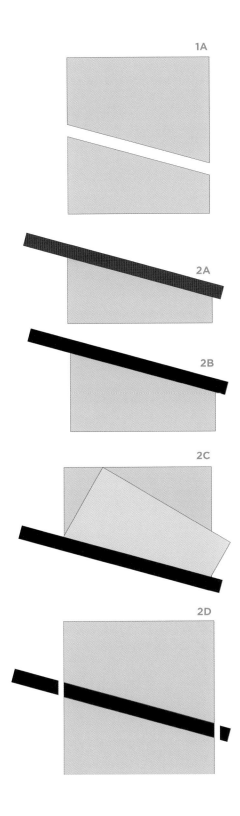

1 slice

Using a rotary cutter and ruler, slice a 10" square once on a slight diagonal. Stay at least 2" away from the top and bottom edge of the block as you make the cut. **1A**

2 stitch

After the block has been sliced, place a black 1½" strip atop one part of the block with right sides facing. Notice that the strip extends about ¼" – ½" beyond the edge, allowing for the angle as well as the ¼" seam allowance. Stitch in place. **2A**

Press the seam allowance to "set" it after stitching. Do not trim yet. **2B**

Place the remaining half of the block on the other side of the strip with right sides facing. Stitch it to the strip. You are working at an angle, so the edges of the new piece will extend past the pieces that have already been stitched. **2C**

Press the block open with the seam allowances going toward the black strip. Trim the remainder of the strip off. You should have enough left over to complete at least **2 more blocks**. **2D**

Repeat the instructions and make **41 more blocks**. Don't try to

place the strip in the same place or at the same angle. With more variation, you can achieve more interest, movement and fun!

3 trim

After all blocks have been made, trim each to **9½" square**.

4 arrange

Place the blocks on a design wall with **6 blocks across and 7 blocks down**. Arrange the colors to your satisfaction. You might try using the darker colors on the outside edges and the brightest ones in the center. Switch them around until you're happy.

Be careful that the black strips don't make joining lines through the quilt. You might want to rotate a block 90 degrees occasionally so the line is running in a different direction.

Once you are satisfied with the arrangement of your blocks, stitch them together into **rows of 6. Make 7 rows.** Press the seam allowances of the even numbered rows toward the right and the odd numbered rows toward the left.

5 border

Stitch (7) 1½" x WOF strips together end-to-end to make one long strip. Trim the borders from this strip.

1. Using your rotary cutter and ruler, slice a 10″ square apart at a slight angle.

2. Place a 1½″ black strip atop one of the pieces with right sides facing. Stitch in place.

3. Place the remaining piece of the block on the other side of the strip and stitch it in place.

4. Open the block, press and square to 9½″.

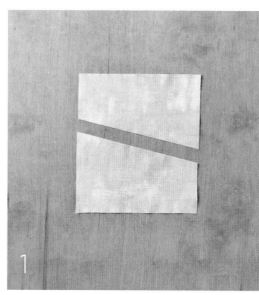

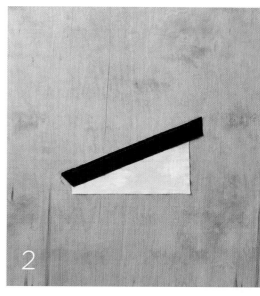

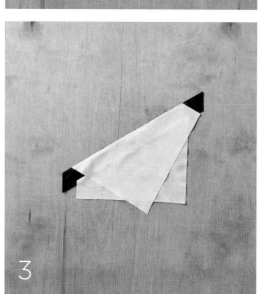

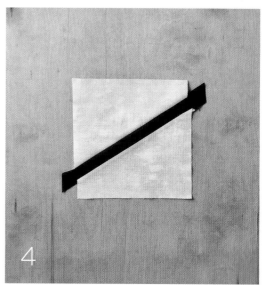

Measure the quilt through the center vertically. Cut two strips approximately 63½" and sew one to each side of the quilt top.

Measure the quilt through the center horizontally and cut two strips that measurement, approximately 56½". Sew one strip to the top and the other to the bottom.

6 quilt and bind

Layer the quilt with batting and backing and quilt. There is a lot of negative space, so have fun! After the quilting is complete, square up the quilt and trim away all excess batting and backing. Add binding to complete the quilt.

▶ twin sisters
sara gallegos

My love of quilting began in my early 20's when my mother opened up a quilt shop. It was a marvelous place to be. Mom, Grandma, and I had so much fun ordering fabrics and digging into the boxes as soon as they would arrive at the shop. That shop is now closed but I have since opened another quilt shop with my stepmom, Mary, called Decorative Stitch.

Now, I often have my two daughters at the shop with me, and they're growing up to love fabric just like I did. My girls get just as excited as I do to open up new fabric shipments and fold the beautiful yardage into delicious fat quarters, just waiting to be made into a quilt. Quilting is a labor of love and it warms my heart to have learned this hobby from Mom, Grandma, and countless other teachers. I am so grateful that I am able to continue sharing my passion with my stepmom, friends, students, and, most of all, my daughters.

Creating a quilt for Modblock was a thrilling experience for me. I immediately started binge watching Missouri Star Quilt Company tutorials to find the perfect inspiration piece. While I got inspired and laughed along with Jenny, I kept searching for the perfect block that reached out to me on a personal level. Once I saw the Jack and Jill tutorial using the "Twin Sisters" block, I knew this was the quilt for me! Although my daughters aren't twins, it reminds me of them. They're quite the pair! They bring joy, inspiration, and laughter to my world every single day. So I set out to find just the right fabric to create a fun quilt for us to take on our many adventures together.

▶ mix it up

The next time you go to a quilt shop, take a deeper look around and instead of going straight for the fabric you typically choose, see what else draws you in. Use your imagination to discern what that fabric should be. Some fabrics are more suited to certain shapes, and even the size of the print can determine the size of the quilt block. Let the fabric tell you what it should become.

you've got this

"Twin Sisters" is a quick and easy block to put together, plus it's a lot of fun! There aren't too many seams to match, so your sewing doesn't have to be perfect. It would be an excellent quilt for a beginner.

▸ supply list

makes a 77½″ X 88¼″ quilt

QUILT TOP
- 1 print fat quarter bundle – must have a minimum of 15 pieces
- 3 yards background fabric

INNER BORDER
- ¾ yard

OUTER BORDER
- 1¼ yards

BACKING
- 7 yards

SAMPLE QUILT
- **Pacific** by Elizabeth Hartman

▸ *visit msqc.co/modblock2 for tutorials & info on how to make this quilt.*

2A

2B

2C

3A

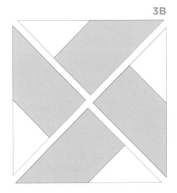
3B

1 cut

From each of 11 fat quarters, cut:

- (4) 4½ x 18" strips

From the background fabric, cut:

- (22) 4½" strips across the width of the fabric - Subcut each strip in half on the fold line of the fabric (depending on the width of the fabric, the strip will measure approximately 4½" x 20" - 22").

2 sew and cut

Sew a background 4½" strip to a print 4½" strip. **2A**

Cut 2 matching strip sets each into (2) 8½" squares for a total of 4 squares. **2B**

Cut the squares from corner to corner once on the diagonal.

▶ **NOTE** *All squares must be cut in the same direction. After cutting the four squares, you will have enough triangles to make two blocks.* **2C**

3 make blocks

Select 4 matching triangles that are primarily background and sew them together as shown. Notice the background pieces form an X. **Make 21. 3A**

Select 4 matching triangles that are primarily print and sew them together as shown. Notice the print pieces make up the X. **Make 21. 3B**

4 arrange in rows

Arrange the blocks into rows. Alternate the blocks that have a print X in the center with a block that has a background X in the center. Make **7 rows** with each row having **6 blocks.** Sew the rows together once you are happy with the placement of the blocks.

5 inner border

Cut (8) 2½" strips across the width of the fabric. Sew the strips together end-to-end to make one long strip. Trim the borders from this strip.

Refer to Borders (pg. 103) in the Construction Basics to measure and cut the inner borders. The strips are approximately 75¾" for the sides and approximately 69" for the top and bottom.

6 outer border

Cut (8) 5" strips across the width of the fabric. Sew the strips together end-to-end to make one long strip. Trim the borders from this strip.

Refer to Borders (pg. 103) in the Construction Basics to measure and cut the inner borders. The strips are

1 Sew a 4½" background strip to a 4½" print strip. Cut the sewn strip into 8½" squares.

2 Cut the squares from corner to corner once on the diagonal. All squares need to be cut in the same direction.

3 Select 4 matching triangles that are primarily background and sew them together as shown. Notice that the background pieces form an X.

4 Sew 4 matching triangles together that are primarily print. Notice the print pieces form an X.

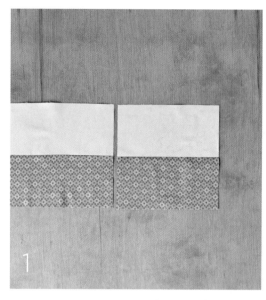

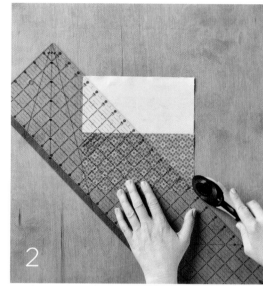

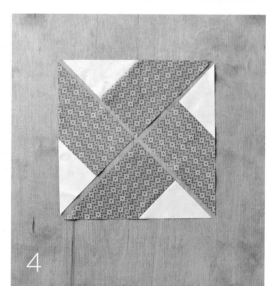

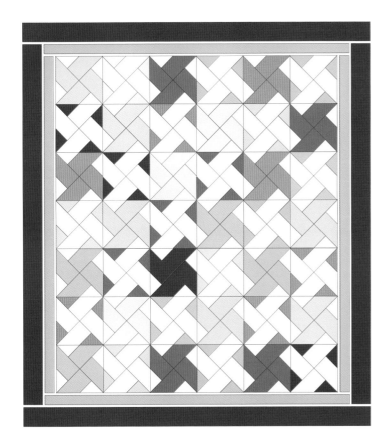

approximately 79¾" for the sides and approximately 78" for the top and bottom.

7 quilt and bind

Layer the quilt with batting and backing and quilt. After the quilting is complete, square up the quilt and trim away all excess batting and backing. Measure and add together the width and length of your quilt and multiply that number by 2. Add 10" to that number. That should be the length of the binding you will need.

Cut enough 2½" strips from the remaining pieces of fat quarters and sew them end-to-end using a mitered seam to equal your measurement. (You'll want to measure the length of binding after you've stitched all the pieces together.) Bind your quilt using your favorite method or refer to the Construction Basics (pg. 104) for instructions.

modern courthouse
christopher thompson

Before I could even walk and talk, I could be found playing under a quilt frame. All my life, I've been surrounded by family members who've taught me to love tinkering with crafts, quilting, and pursuing other creative endeavors.

This early creative beginning led me to a career in fashion, but as the years went by, my passion for quilting emerged once more and I couldn't ignore it! I fell in love with the modern quilting movement and it's been on my mind nonstop ever since! Art, music, fashion, and the world around me are my biggest influences, but I'll never forget where I came from. This quilt project is a combination of my love of modern quilting, with a nod to my traditional roots.

Quilts have come a long way since their original function, to keep us nice and toasty. Of course we still use them to adorn our beds and cuddle up with, but they've become a beautiful form of inspiration as well. Mini quilts seem to serve no utilitarian function, but they are very popular in the world of modern quilting. These fun, quick projects can help you explore new quilting techniques, change up a color palette, or work out an idea that could grow into a larger quilt. Playing with quilt shapes in mini form also allows you to take more modern format risks. And now that I'm thinking about it, they do have many functional uses! They can be used as mug rugs, potholders, pillow covers, and even small crib quilts. What else can you think of?

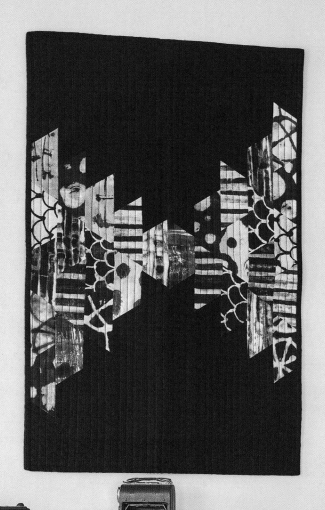

endless possibilities

This particular mini quilt takes its inspiration from a traditional courthouse steps quilt block, which is a variation on the log cabin block. There are many ways to play with this traditional pattern. You can create so different designs with this seemingly simple block.

negative or positive

Notice how using a white background, instead of black, changes the effect of the quilt completely. Black puts more emphasis on the patterned pieces while white gives the edges a sharper contrast. Either way, you can't lose!

▸ supply list

makes a 20" X 28" quilt

QUILT TOP
- 1 package 5" print squares
- ¾ yard Black (Moda Bella solids)

BORDER
- ¼ yard coordinating fabric

BACKING
- ⅞ yard coordinating fabric

BINDING
- ⅞ yard coordinating fabric

ADDITIONAL TOOLS
- 1 MSQC 5" Half-Hexagon Template

SAMPLE QUILT
- **Black + White** by Marcia Derse for Windham Fabrics
- **Black Moda Bella solid** by Moda Fabrics

▸ *visit msqc.co/modblock2 for tutorials & info on how to make this quilt.*

1A

1 cut

From the 5″ print squares, cut:

- (30) half-hexagons using the MSQC Half-Hexagon template.

From the black fabric, cut:

- (10) 2½″ strips across the width of the fabric.

Subcut the strips into

- (20) 2½″ x 18″ strips - trim one end of 10 strips on a 60 degree angle using your rotary cutter and mat. Trim the remaining 10 strips the other direction. **1B**

▶ **TIP** *Use the same fabric collection or mix it up for something new and interesting. You can also use the MSQC half-hexagon die for Sizzix, which is what we used.*

▶ **NOTE** *You can cut 2 half-hexagons from each square* **1A** *but if you cut one shape from each, you will have a larger variety in your quilt.*

▶ **TIP** *You can also use a roll of 2½″ strips for the background pieces. Place one end of your strip on the 60 degree and 0″ intersection on your mat and cut. It comes out perfect each time!*

2 arrange and sew

Refer to the diagram and sew the half-hexagon shapes together into rows, adding a background strip on either end of each row. Press the seam allowances open. **2A**

Sew each row together, pressing your seams toward the background. Notice that we decided to flip the rows to achieve an asymmetrical effect. **2B**

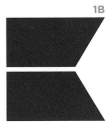

1B

2A

1 Trim the black strips using either the half-hexagon template or your rotary cutting ruler and mat at the necessary 60-degree angle

.

2 Lay out the half-hexagons and strips as shown.

3 Sew the pieces together.

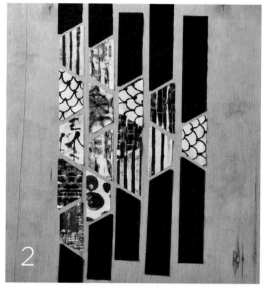

2B

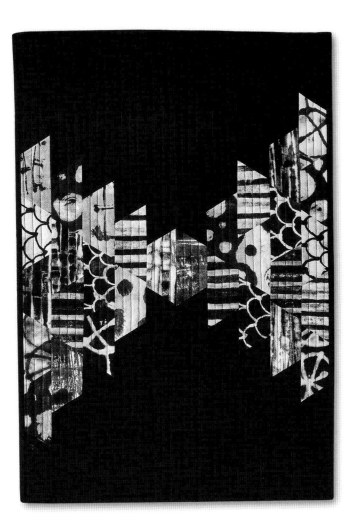

▶ **TIP** *As you add the background strips, the rows will get longer. That's okay, you can square it up at the end.*

Trim the quilt top the way you like. In the sample quilt, we trimmed it down to 20½″ by 28½″.

3 quilt and bind
Layer the quilt top, batting and backing. Quilt as you please. Square up the quilt and add binding to finish. We cut the binding for this quilt 2¼″ wide. See the Construction Basics on page 104 for binding instructions.

reference

Boxed Weave 65" X 82"

Designed/Natalie Earnheart Pieced/Kelly McKenzie & Cindy Morris

Quilted/Debbie Allen & Raven Rhoads

QUILT TOP
- 1 package 10" squares
- 3½ yards background fabric – includes inner border
  (Cotton Supreme Solids Optical White 9617 33T)

BORDER
- 1¼ yards

BACKING
- 5 yards

ADDITIONAL TOOLS
- 1 MSQC 10" Half Hexagon Template

SAMPLE QUILT
- Cat Lady by Sara Watts for Cotton+Steel

QUILTING PATTERN
- Water

Cornerstone 74" X 88"

Designed/Amy Ellis Pieced/Amy Ellis Quilted/Mari Zullig

QUILT TOP
- 15 fat quarters
- 5 yards Eggshell (Moda Bella solid 9900 281)

BACKING
- 5¼ yards

BINDING
- ⅔ yard

SAMPLE QUILT
- Serenity by Amy Ellis for Moda Fabrics
- Bella Solids Eggshell (9900 281) by Moda Fabrics

QUILTING PATTERN
- Champagne Bubbles

Light Box   44" X 40½"

Designed/Pieced/Quilted by/ Christopher Thompson

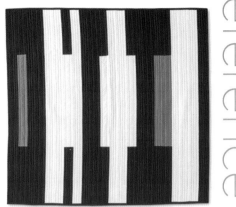

QUILT TOP
- ¼ yard Azalea (Moda Bella solid 9900 144)
- 1 yard White (Moda Bella solid 9900 98)
- 1½ yard Black (Moda Bella solid 9900 99) - includes binding

BACKING
- 1½ yards

BACKING
- 3 yards coordinating fabric

SAMPLE QUILT
- Bella Solids by Moda Fabric

Modern Courthouse   20" X 28"

Designed/Pieced/Quilted/ Christopher Thompson

QUILT TOP
- 1 package 5" print squares
- ¾ yard black (Moda Bella solid 9900 99)

BORDER
- ¼ yard coordinating fabric

BACKING
- ⅞ yard coordinating fabric

BINDING
- ⅞ yard coordinating fabric

ADDITIONAL TOOLS
- 1 MSQC 5" Half-Hexagon Template

SAMPLE QUILT
- Black + White by Marcia Derse for Windham Fabrics
- Black Moda Bella solid by Moda Fabrics (9900 99)

reference

Moonlight 68" X 82"

Designed/Pieced/Victoria Findlay Wolfe Quilted/Abigail Anderson

QUILT TOP
- 5½ yards Pacific Blue – includes border and binding (K001-90)
- ¾ yard Honeysuckle (K001-490)
- ½ yard Peach (K001-1281)
- ¼ yard Torch (K001-450)

BACKING
- 4¼ yards Hot Pink

SAMPLE QUILT
- Kona Solids by Robert Kaufman

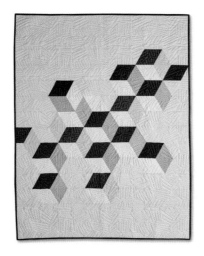

Rhombus Dance 52" X 65"

Designed/Christine Ricks Pieced/Cindy Morris Quilted/Betty Bates

QUILT TOP
RJR Cotton Supreme Solids
- ½ yard Elephantastic Pink (RJR-9617-277)
- ¼ yard Paris (RJR-9617-235 RP)
- ½ yard Tickled Pink (RJR-9617-330)
- ½ yard Tiffany Box (RJR-9617-291)
- 1¼ yards Bayou (RJR-9617-344)
- ½ yard Navy (RJR-9617-30T)
- 2½ yards On The Rocks
  (RJR-9617-283)

BACKING
- 3½ yards

BINDING
- ¾ yard

ADDITIONAL TOOLS
- MSQC Rhombus Template

SAMPLE QUILT
- RJR Cotton Supreme Solids

QUILTING PATTERN
- Aztec

Rising Star 57" X 66½"
Designed/Ron Doan Pieced/Carol Henderson
Quilted/Linda Frump

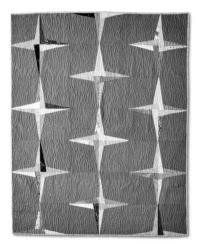

QUILT TOP
- 1 roll of 2½" strips
- 1 package of 10" squares (42 count)

BACKING
- 3¾ yards

BINDING
- ¾ yard

SAMPLE QUILT
- Carkai by Carolyn Friedlander for Robert Kauffman
- Kona Cotton Steel Yardage by Robert Kaufman

QUILTING PATTERN
- Flame

Slice-A-Block 56" X 65"
Designed/Pieced/Quilted/ Rob Appell

QUILT TOP
- 1 package of 10" squares (42 count)
- (1) 1½" roll black strips

BACKING & BINDING
- 4 yards Kona Black

SAMPLE QUILT
- Grunge by Moda Fabrics
- Bella Solids Black

reference

Tiny Wonky Stars 69" X 81"

Designed/Jenny Doan Pieced/Carol Henderson
Quilted/Abigail Anderson

QUILT TOP
- 1 roll of 2½" print strips
- 5¼ yards background fabric – includes borders
  (Bella Solids Bleached White 9900 98)

BACKING
- 5 yards

BINDING
- ¾ yard

SAMPLE QUILT
- Essential Magic Colors by Wilmington Prints
- Bella Solids Bleached White (9900 98)

QUILTING PATTERN
- Playing Angles

Twin Sister 72½" X 88¼"

Designed/Pieced/Quilted/ Sara Gallegos

QUILT TOP
- 1 print fat quarter bundle – must have a minimum of 15 pieces
- 3 yards background fabric

INNER BORDER
- ¾ yard

OUTER BORDER
- 1¼ yards

BACKING
- 7 yards

SAMPLE QUILT
- Pacific Cool by Elizabeth Hartman and Solids

QUILTING PATTERN
- Squares

construction basics

- All seams are ¼" inch unless directions specify differently.

- Cutting instructions are given at the point when cutting is required.

- Precuts are not prewashed; therefore do not prewash other fabrics in the project

- All strips are cut WOF

- Remove all selvages

- All yardages based on 42" WOF

ACRONYMS USED

MSQC	Missouri Star Quilt Co.
RST	right sides together
WST	wrong sides together
HST	half-square triangle
WOF	width of fabric
LOF	length of fabric

pre-cut glossary

5" SQUARE PACK
1 = (42) 5" squares or ¾ yd of fabric
1 = baby
2 = crib
3 = lap
4 = twin

2½" STRIP ROLL
1 = (40) 2½" strip roll cut the width of fabric
    or 2¾ yds of fabric
1 = a twin
2 = queen

10" SQUARE PACK
1 = (42) 10" square pack of fabric: 2¾ yds total
1 = a twin
2 = queen

When we mention a precut, we are basing the pattern on a 40-42 count pack. Not all precuts have the same count, so be sure to check the count on your precut to make sure you have enough pieces to complete your project.

general quilting

- All seams are ¼" inch unless directions specify differently.
- Cutting instructions are given at the point when cutting is required.
- Precuts are not prewashed; therefore do not prewash other fabrics in the project.
- All strips are cut width of fabric.
- Remove all selvages.
- All yardages based on 42" width of fabric (WOF).

press seams

- Use the cotton setting on your iron when pressing.
- Press the seam just as it was sewn RST. This "sets" the seam.
- To set the seam, press just as it was sewn with right sides together.
- With dark fabric on top, lift the dark fabric and press back.
- The seam allowance is pressed toward the dark side. Some patterns may direct otherwise for certain situations.
- Press toward borders. Pieced borders may demand otherwise.
- Press diagonal seams open on binding to reduce bulk.

borders

- Always measure the quilt top 3 times before cutting borders.
- Start measuring about 4" in from each side and through the center vertically.
- Take the average of those 3 measurements.
- Cut 2 border strips to that size. Piece strips together if needed.
- Attach one to either side of the quilt.
- Position the border fabric on top as you sew. The feed dogs can act like rufflers. Having the border on top will prevent waviness and keep the quilt straight.
- Repeat this process for the top and bottom borders, measuring the width 3 times.
- Include the newly attached side borders in your measurements.
- Press toward the borders.

binding

find a video tutorial at: www.msqc.co/006

- Use 2½" strips for binding.
- Sew strips end-to-end into one long strip with diagonal seams, aka plus sign method (next). Press seams open.
- Fold in half lengthwise wrong sides together and press.
- The entire length should equal the outside dimension of the quilt plus 15" - 20."

plus sign method

- Lay one strip across the other as if to make a plus sign right sides together.
- Sew from top inside to bottom outside corners crossing the intersections of fabric as you sew. Trim excess to ¼" seam allowance.
- Press seam open.

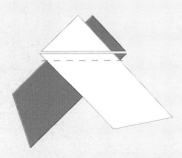

attach binding

- Match raw edges of folded binding to the quilt top edge.
- Leave a 10" tail at the beginning.
- Use a ¼" seam allowance.
- Start in the middle of a long straight side.

find a video tutorial at: www.msqc.co/001

10" tail   ¼"

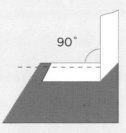

90°

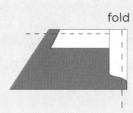

fold

miter corners

- Stop sewing ¼" before the corner.
- Move the quilt out from under the presser foot.
- Clip the threads.
- Flip the binding up at a 90˚ angle to the edge just sewn.
- Fold the binding down along the next side to be sewn, aligning raw edges.
- The fold will lie along the edge just completed.
- Begin sewing on the fold.

close binding

*MSQC recommends **The Binding Tool** from TQM Products to finish binding perfectly every time.*

- Stop sewing when you have 12" left to reach the start.
- Where the binding tails come together, trim excess leaving only 2½" of overlap.
- It helps to pin or clip the quilt together at the two points where the binding starts and stops. This takes the pressure off of the binding tails while you work.
- Use the plus sign method to sew the two binding ends together, except this time when making the plus sign, match the edges. Using a pencil, mark your sewing line because you won't be able to see where the corners intersect. Sew across.

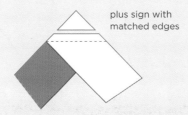

plus sign with matched edges

- Trim off excess; press seam open.
- Fold in half wrong sides together, and align all raw edges to the quilt top.
- Sew this last binding section to the quilt. Press.
- Turn the folded edge of the binding around to the back of the quilt and tack into place with an invisible stitch or machine stitch if you wish.